Be Kind

Mind Your Manners

By Kimberly M. Anderson

BE KIND MIND YOUR MANNERS
By Kimberly M. Anderson

@2019 Kimberly M. Anderson

Illustrations by Mark Nunn
Book Design by Helen L. Barrios

Library of Congress Control Number 2019900216
ISBN-13   978-0-578-44165-8

All rights reserved. No part of this book may be reproduced or transmitted in any form or by means, graphic, electronic, or mechanical, including, photocopying, recording, taping, or by any information storage retrieval system, without permission of the author.

Published by
Kimberly M. Anderson, M.Ed., MS

Thank you for always supporting me, Gina!
To my cousin Babe and Helen tell Daddy, hi!

Dear Parents,

Parents are teachers too!
Your child's love for reading can start with you. You can help your child develop healthy social skills while increasing their literacy skills by reading with them daily.

Reading is a never ending cycle of life. It is a fundamental tool that will be used throughout the life span of a person. Encouraging your child to read at an early age can help develop positive self-confidence. The more your child reads, it can expand their mind to a lifetime of limitless possibilities.

Be Kind Mind Your Manners is a book created to promote positive learning for children.

It is a timeless book that can be used to guide reading for early emergent, emergent, and fluent readers.
In addition, the social skills at the back of the book can be learned, assessed and applied by parents, teachers, and/or mental health professionals by completing the activities at the end of the story.

ENJOY READING!

Alaya and Zoey are on their way to school. Alaya and Zoey love to listen to music together. As usual, Alaya likes to tell her mom to turn the radio up louder so she and Zoey can sing along with the music. While riding in the car, Alaya's mother explained the importance of having great manners. "Alaya, it is very important for you to be polite to others," said mom.

"I will remember what you told us, and I will try to teach others today at school," said Alaya.

Alaya and Zoey made it to school. They walked in the classroom. Their teacher greeted them with a big smile. "Hello and good morning children! Welcome to 2nd grade," said their teacher!

They walked into the class and noticed their clothes were different than the other children. Everyone began to stare at them and laugh. Alaya became very sad, but she remembered what her mom told her.

Alaya said, "I like my clothes and it is ok to be different!" Zoey said, "it is not kind to laugh at someone because they are different!" The class said, "we are sorry Alaya and Zoey."

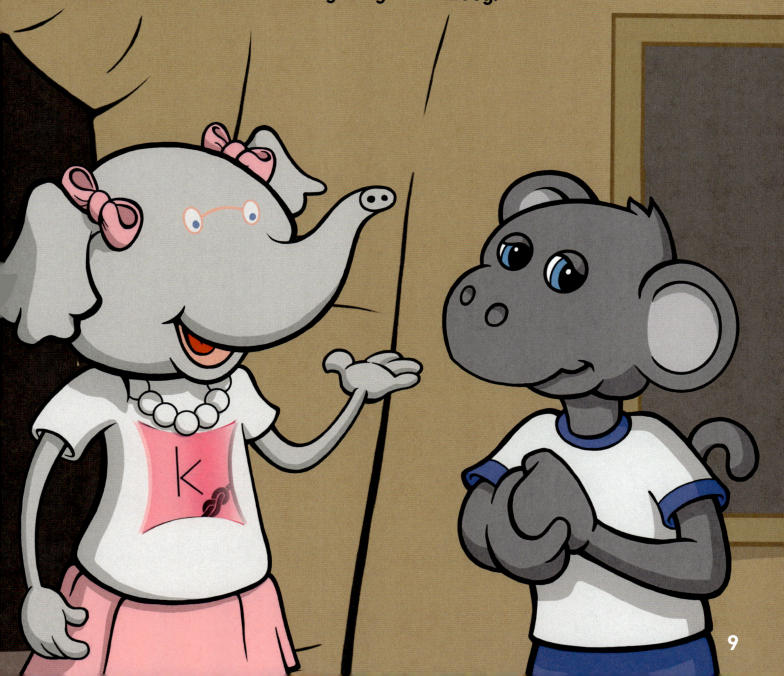

The morning announcements began over the school intercom. Alaya and Zoey were excited to hear what they were going to eat for lunch. Some of the children in the class continued talking during the announcements.

After the announcements were over, the teacher told the class the importance of listening. She also explained that when you don't listen, you could miss out on learning something important.

The principal Mrs. Brewer stopped by to visit their teacher. Two boys in class kept calling out the teacher's name while she was talking to the principal. Zoey and Alaya were very quiet.

After the principal left, the teacher explained to the students that they should raise their hands and wait when adults or other people are talking.

The teacher had the students line up to take a restroom break. She had everyone line up by their last name. One student tried to cut Alaya in line while headed to the restroom.

Alaya told the student, "it's not nice to cut people in line." The students went into the restroom one at a time.

As they came out, the teacher reminded the students to wash their hands after they use the restroom. She told them that they could get sick or spread germs if they did not wash their hands.

It was time for lunch. "I'm hungry Alaya," said Zoey.

As the other children were in line, they noticed some students were cutting others. The teacher told the students, "you have to be patient and wait your turn, pushing is not going to get us to lunch quicker and someone could get hurt."

All the students then formed a straight line.

While they were eating lunch, several of the children were burping. Alaya told the children, "you need to say excuse me after you burp!"

After lunch, it was time to go to recess. Several of the students wanted to play four square, other students wanted to play on the jungle gym. A few of the girls even jumped rope. Some students did not want to share the jump rope with Alaya and Zoey.
Alaya and Zoey said,
"we all must take turns."

At the end of the day, the teacher assigned everyone a job task to clean the classroom. Some of the students had to stack the chairs and others were responsible for picking things up from the floor.

The teacher began sorting the kids by the way they should go home. As the teacher called the students home for dismissal, Alaya could not hear the teacher's voice. The teacher told the class "we should not talk while the teacher is talking, that's not nice!" Alaya's teacher thanked her for helping her with the students.

Alaya's mother picked Zoey and her up at the end of the day. Alaya's mother asked her, "how was your day?" "I remembered what you taught me mom about manners and I decided to share with the class today." "That's great," said Alaya's mother, "I'm so happy you enjoyed your first day."

Be Kind

Activities and Role Playing

Activity 1– Practicing Your Manners

Activity Instructions:
Manners are the way people are supposed to behave and act at school or in their community. After you have completed each task, discuss or role play each scenario with a parent, teacher, or mental health professional.

- ✓ Say please and thank you
- ✓ Be respectful when an adult is talking
- ✓ Say please when requesting something
- ✓ Wait on your turn to speak
- ✓ Give someone a compliment
- ✓ Say excuse me
- ✓ Take turns sharing at home or at school
- ✓ Give an apology when needed

Well Done! You super star!

Activity 2 – Monitor Your Manners

Activity Instructions:
Look through a magazine for people using good manners and being kind. Draw pictures below to illustrate what you have found in the magazine. Discuss the images with a parent, teacher, or mental health professional.

Activity 3 – Being Helpful

Change can begin with YOU!

Activity Instructions:
Everyone likes to be around a person that helps other people. Check of the list of things that interest you and write about how you can create change in your community.

- [ ] World Hunger _____
- [ ] World Poverty _____
- [ ] Animals _____
- [ ] Literacy _____
- [ ] Healthy Lifestyles _____
- [ ] Helping the Homeless _____
- [ ] World Peace _____
- [ ] Cultural Diversity _____
- [ ] Others _____
- [ ] I Can Change the World by _____

_____

_____

_____

_____

Literacy Activities

Comprehension Checklist

Think about what you have read in the story Be Kind Mind Your Manners.
Use the pictures in the story to help you find out the questions listed below.

Talk about what happened first in the story. _____
_____

Then what happened next? _____
_____

What happened at the end of the story? What was the problem in the story? _____
_____

What was the most important idea in this book? _____
_____

Retell the most important events in your own words. _____
_____

Career Spotlight

What does an author do in a book?
_____

What does an illustrator do in a book?
_____

What was the author's purpose for writing the book?
_____

Graphic Organizer
Story Elements: Complete the fields in the blank.

Setting	Characters

Problem	Solution

Beginning	Middle	End

Favorite Part

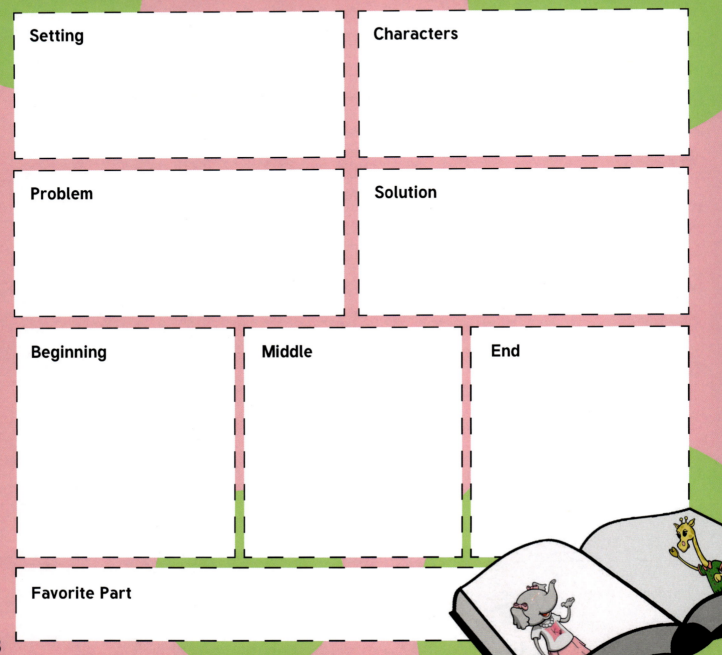

Graphic Organizer

Compare and Contrast:
Think about what you have read in the story Be Kind Mind Your Manners to help you fill in the circles. This lesson is a tool to examine the differences between elephants and giraffes. In addition, it could also be great for studying safari habitats for animals. After you have completed the lesson, discuss the similarities and differences.

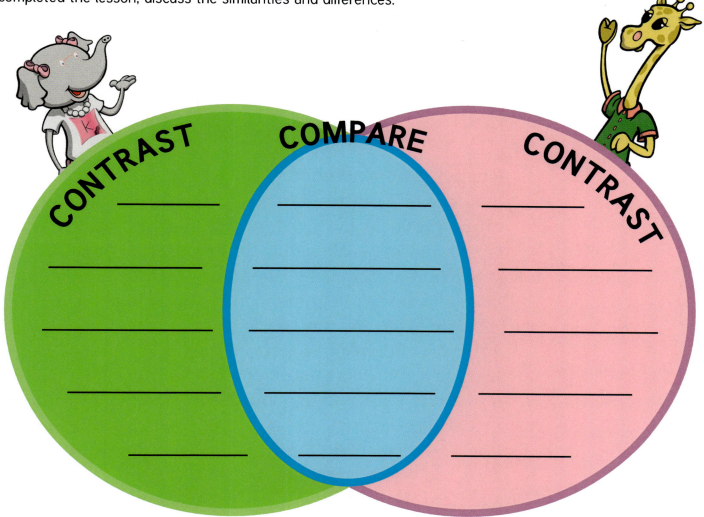

Show how two or more things are alike and/or how they are different.

Meet the Author

Kimberly M. Anderson is a proud second generation graduate of Langston University, she earned a Master of Education in Elementary Education and Master of Counseling in Rehabilitation Counseling. She is a second generation educator and continues to work in the mental health field. She is a proud member of the Alpha Kappa Alpha Sorority, Inc. and the Order of the Eastern Star. In 2017, she authored her first children's book entitled Be Kind which encourages parent-child participation and introduces a variety of thoughts, feelings, and social skills, that can be learned, assessed, and applied by parents, teachers, or mental health professionals. On April 12, 2008 she was honored for D.E.A.R. (Drop Everything and Read) Day at the Oklahoma State Capitol. Kimberly still works to improve literacy in the state of Oklahoma.

Made in the USA
Monee, IL
11 October 2020

44520474R00019